# Becoming Best Friends -

## Safe Play!

## Children and Dogs Together

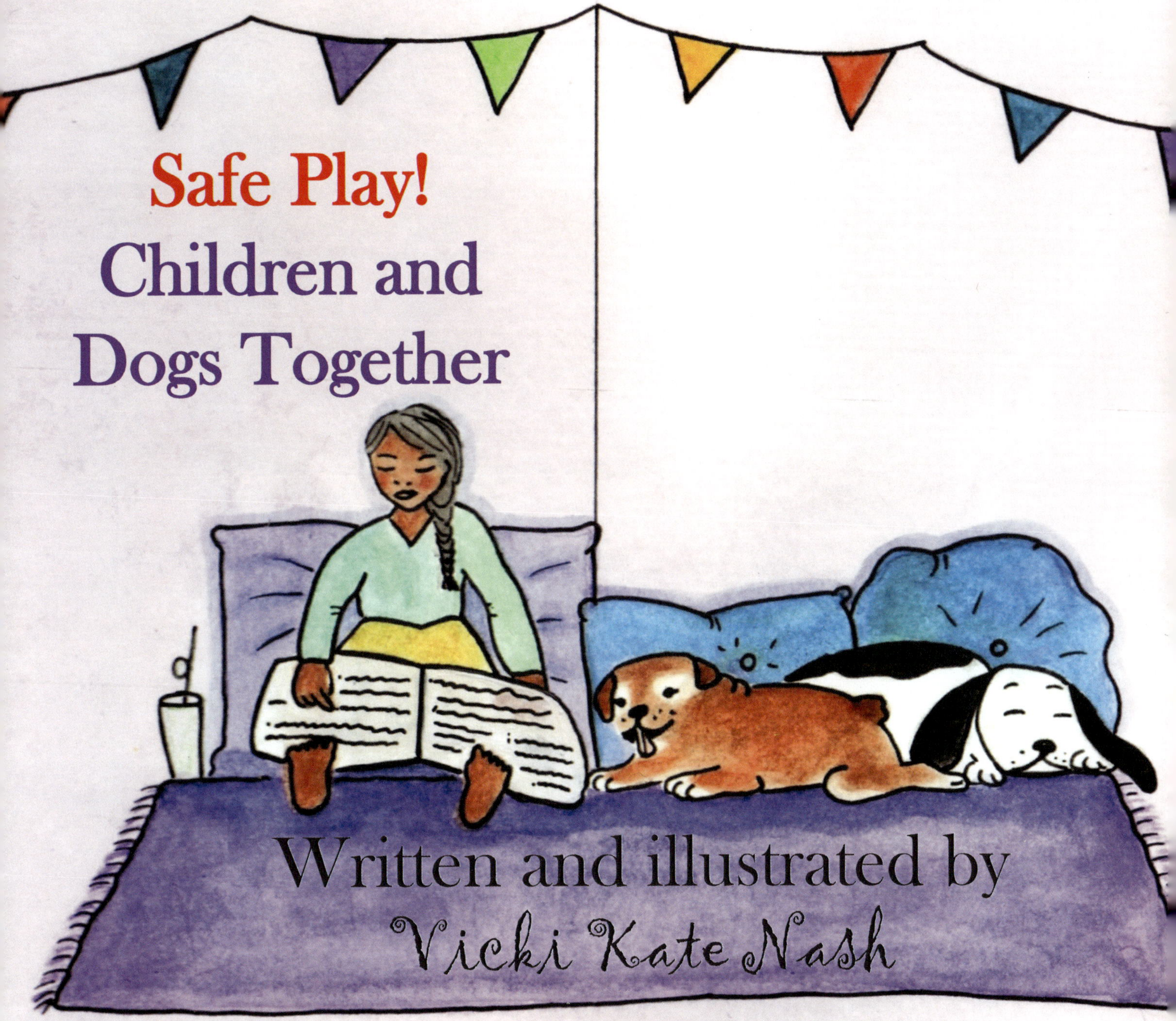

Written and illustrated by

Vicki Kate Nash

vickikatenash@gmail.com
ISBN: 978-0-9956695-5-0

For H, L and
Millie.

# This book belongs to

..........................................................

What could we do
together for fun?

I **love** to go for walks with you and run about!

I love it when you talk,
not shout.

Trips to the woods make me **feel** so good!

I love to play each day with you. I even love to chew your shoe! I love to play each day, balls and frisbees along the way.

I can play and sleep, ALL day!

Trips to the beach and hide-and-seek!

Running, digging, swimming.

Keeping cool!

# What am I saying? I have feelings too, just like you...

**Loose, wiggly body. Big smile!**

**Play bow!**

**Wide smile, wide, relaxed eyes and body.**

**Large grin, relaxed, happy face. Wiggly, loose tongue.**

I am happy! I am ready to play!

# *Some* ways I can show you, I'm not very sure...

Just like you, when I am worried or scared, I can fidget and fiddle. To calm myself down.

When I am cross, I can tell you by growling. This *usually* means please **STOP!** I don't like that.

Be still like a tree. You will then be quite boring to the dog. Keep calm and still.

Fold your arms and ignore silly behaviour. Move **slowly** away.

# Meet and greet...
# How does this dog feel?

Check back on the body language (doggy language) pages.

This dog is tied up and is without its owner. Always stop, look and think. Always ask the owner if you may touch the dog, then check...how do you think the dog is feeling? Worried or happy?

It may be best to wait. Next time, walk up slowly and calmly. Ask the owner first and always give the dog space to move away.

Approach slowly sideways, like a crab! This is much less scary for a dog than rushing up face first. Give **space**.

**Space** for you! And **space** for the dog.

# At meal, or snack times...

Give me **space**, to finish what's on my plate. Please don't touch, or take my food. It could put me in a bad mood!

Let me rest and I will soon be back to my best...

Giving me **space**, away from my face. (Never try to wake a sleeping dog). I dream just like you.

# Dogs with jobs...

## Guide Dogs for the Blind.

A Guide Dog keeps their blind, or partially sighted owner safe.
Safely guiding the way...

Dogs are superheroes!

# Hearing Dogs for deaf people...

Using their amazing super senses, these clever dogs alert their owner to the sound of the doorbell, alarm clock, or even the smoke alarm!

# Dogs for Good...

Assistance dogs support adults and children with a range of disabilities. They also support children with autism.

## Dogs are good!

Police dogs are specially trained to help the police.

Search and Rescue Dogs help find trapped, or lost people...

Best friends, together at the park!

Going home, before it gets too dark.

# Becoming best friends...

What do I need to keep me happy and healthy?
I *love* it when you spend time with me.
Healthy food, exercise and company.
Fresh water and a warm and cosy bed.
Somewhere soft to lay my head.
A bond to remember *forever.*
Dogs are good!

Children and dogs can build a strong bond. They can learn mutual respect and an understanding of each other. *Safe and fun interactions.*

*Children and dogs should always be supervised.*

Dogs are good!
Good bye!

# Other books by Vicki Kate Nash...

21658885R00021

Printed in Poland
by Amazon Fulfillment
Poland Sp. z o.o., Wrocław